Public Speaking: Tips On Overcoming Fear And Presentations

By

Jamal Williams

Version 1.1 – May 2016

Published by Jamal Williams at KDP

Contents

Public Speaking: Tips On Overcoming Fear And Presentations

Chapter 1

Get Paid For Speaking

Traditions, gatherings, meetings, and travels are a blasting business nowadays. Occasion organizers are profiting, and they require you to help them fill void speaker spaces. You must make sense of how you can properly fit into these timetables.

Look at associations, for example, the Voyage Lines Global Affiliation, the Universal Relationship of Tradition and Guests Authorities, and Meeting Organizers Worldwide, which will likely likewise have a neighborhood part in your general vicinity.

Do some exploration to discover what sorts of themes are being examined on the circuit. In what manner would you be able to make a point that is sufficiently new to separate you, however not all that new that you won't fit in?

In case you're experiencing issues settling on the right point for you, attempt to do a study of your physical business sector to figure out what they most need to learn. Make a poll find their requirements, and afterward, know how to fill those necessities.

Turned into a Specialist

When you have decided your theme, you have to build up yourself as an expert. There are a few approaches. You can compose articles and offer them for nothing to proper productions. You can independently publish a book or put a digital book on Cd, which you can then incorporate into your press unit and offer after your discourses.

At whatever point you do make a booking, present an official statement to suitable media outlets declaring your discourse. You can utilize an online administration for this, or you can target particular productions, radio and TV slots. On the off chance that you give radio and TV outlets a singer for their plugs that will make their audience members tune in, you have a vastly improved shot of getting reporting in real time.

Each time you make a booking, approach the customer for referrals!

Tailor Your Theme to Your Group of onlookers

When you get a booking, ensure your material is customized to your group of onlookers. Get some answers concerning the general population who will hear you out. Have they been there, or would they say they are required to be there? What are their ages? What positions do their hold? What do they most need to learn?

Above all, what amount do they think about your subject? While you would prefer not to talk over their heads, you additionally would prefer not to exhaust your gathering of people with data that is necessary learning to them.

Open Speaking Tips

Hone your discourse so anyone might hear, and time it. Have additional data to confer if you wind up with other time than you expected, and comprehend what you can forget if you come up short on time. Coming up short on time is a great deal more probable, and you should have the capacity to cut from the middle keeping in mind the end goal to end your discourse fittingly. You would prefer not to end in the center and have your consummation misfire.

Continuously have another person present you, and dependable compose your presentation. Along these lines, an essential data about you will be granted to the gathering of individuals, and it won't seem like you're singing your gestures of recognition. You will sound noteworthy, and the group of onlookers will quickly be amped up for hearing what you need to say.

Try not to attempt to be clever unless you know for beyond any doubt that you're entertaining. Keep in mind how Johnny Carson dependably had something self-deploring to say after a joke went level? His joke about his awful joke was more amusing than the first joke. In case, you're going to attempt jokes, acquire Johnny's strategy. This will help you to hide any hint of failure face and keep you from getting bothered if nobody giggles.

Stay away from slides with an excessive number of words. Your group of onlookers will read every slide before you get done with portraying it, and this will only make them feel they've hopped in front of you.

Whatever point you pick, grow your mastery significantly promote by perusing and looking into your subject. Learn all that you can. It won't just enhance your discourse; it will expand your certainty and light your enthusiasm considerably further.

Chapter 2

Using Speeches And Presentations

A late study, promoting officials were asked what they considered the comprehensive most imperative business resource for an innovative expert to have other than ability. The greater part of respondents, 55 percent to be precise, said solid presentation skills. Particular industry experience positioned a removed second with 23 percent; just 3 percent referred to administration experience. The review was directed by an independent research firm and included reactions from 200 promoting officials among the main 1,000 U.S. promoting offices.

MBA graduates thought the capacity to discuss viable with someone else was the absolute most valuable ability in their vocation. "Capacity to convey adequately is the most critical ability you can have," says Daybreak Rosenberg McKay, profession arranging guide at About.com, Inc.

We as a whole need to pitch our thoughts and positions. The main issue is that your belief might be justified regardless of a fortune, yet if you can't convey it unmistakably and with the fitting effect your message may get lost or not persuade a crowd of people. Your incredible thought may get to be useless.

Relational abilities are critical and open talking is an obvious need to anybody seeking to an authority position. I have met exceptionally smart individuals that can't adequately impart even essential data to people around them. They are not influential pioneers and are not as fruitful as they could be. Genuinely extraordinary officials and useful group business pioneers are extremely agreeable communicators. They utilize straightforward dialect that the panel of onlookers can identify with. Truth be told I find that the best communicators are ones that utilization the crowd's dialect and expressions. This exclusive bodes well yet is so frequently missed.

1. Consider your gathering of people deliberately. What dialect or language ought to be maintained a strategic distance from? If language is essential (and unequivocally address this), then characterize any irregular or extraordinary terms (maybe more that once).

2. Have a readied presentation for the individual that will present you. The performance ought to express your name, set up validity with a bio that has a fortifying illustration or two and gives the title of the discourse.

3. In your opening let the gathering of people know to what extent the presentation or discussion will last. Fill them in regarding whether there will be an inquiry and answer session toward the end or whether you will be

accessible to answer addresses later. Clarify when and where you will be.

4. If you are going to make a presentation with a slide indicate then utilize this to keep yourself on track yet, don't read your slides and dependable face and look at the group of onlookers. At the point when looking don't key a lot on a particular individual and convey your eye contact about the room.

5. Never apologize for being anxious. It just makes the gathering of people apprehensive and numerous in the group of onlookers would not have taken note.

6. Use connecting with dialect, for example, "Envision if. . ." or "Have you ever considered . . ." or recount a story that catches the consideration of the gathering of people as an opening. I have heard some at Toastmasters allude to these expressions as mesmerizing stems. They don't entrance yet they get the crowd in the inclination or get the gathering of people to feel the tone of the discourse or presentation better.

7. Utilize your voice to accentuate watchwords or expressions. Try not to be monotone - talk with energy.

8. Use non-verbal communication to stress watchwords or key focuses. Rehearse your discourse or presentation

ahead of time to calibrate your non-verbal communication and your movements.

9. Give a synopsis and a solid conclusion. Your outline and conclusion ought to accentuate the real purposes of the presentation or discourse.

10. Try not to leave the podium unattended when wrapped up. Continuously disregard control to the individual running the meeting or the gathering or to the Speaker. The platform should never be left unattended.

Conveying a discourse or having a high-effect presentation is a fundamental expertise in today's dynamic commercial center. With arranging and some practice you can turn out to be great it. Search for chances to talk and present as one of the key things to overcome is an apprehension of speaking. By talking and introducing more your will turn out to be more alright with it.

Chapter 3

Speaking 101

On the off chance that you need to be an actual expert open speaker, you should finish two things: (1) take in the abilities to end up element in front of an audience, and (2) transform your skill into subjects that get bookings. It's that basic ... furthermore, it's that confounded.

Regardless of the fact that you turn into an open incredible speaker, be that as it may, it isn't sufficient. Your discourse subject must offer something of genuine worth to your audience members, and it should be something that individuals will pay to hear and learn.

On the off chance that you need to profit as an open speaker, the primary thing you have to do is make a rundown of what you know. What learning and abilities have you created throughout the years that could be of assistance to a unique number of individuals? What do you realize that others have to know?

Give Your Gathering of people an Advantage

Your theme must have a particular advantage for your crowd, and your title must make that position clear.

Appealing is essential, yet don't lose the power. "The Force of Positive Considering" may not be the world's most sharp title, but rather the group of onlookers knows precisely what they're going to get. Never give up clarity for astuteness.

You additionally should be precise and particular about your real business sector. Make a rundown of associations or organizations that could most utilize your mastery. Ensure you're putting forth them something they require. If you aren't certain how helpful your attitude may be, get your work done. Perused relevant articles, and research the points of different speakers.

Make a Press Unit

With a specific end goal to profit as an expert speaker, you should to either enlist an advertising delegate or turn into your best supporter. This includes advertising. You're calling card will be your "press pack," which ought to incorporate an expert photo of yourself, data about your points, your bio, testimonials or letters of suggestion, reprints of articles you've composed, a video of a talking engagement, and any media clippings and public statements.

Obviously, in case you're simply beginning, you may need to make a "sham" video. You needn't present a whole discourse in the video, however, ensure it looks proficient.

What's more, dependably send a customized introductory letter with your press unit!

Other than your physical press pack, you will require a site to serve as your "online media group." Add gushing video to your web page, and make a business card with your website address.

The Force of Systems Administration

Systems management is inherently imperative. Give out your business card, and direct individuals to your site. Tell everybody you meet that you're a speaker, and get them amped up for your points. Inquire as to whether they know any individual who might be intrigued. Give them 2 or 3 of your business cards, and request that they pass them along. If you can allude somebody to every individual's business, take an additional business card of theirs also. Apparently, catch up and do as you guarantee, staying in contact with the general population you meet.

Initially, you will probably need to get the majority of your bookings yourself. Speaker's dressers and specialists more often than not work just with speakers who have a long reputation. Make contacts at whatever point conceivable, and send your press unit to your prospects. Make something free that your new prospects can arrange from your site, or encase a postpaid return postcard with your press pack. You can offer a little booklet with data applicable to your theme or a Compact disc containing a short Powerpoint presentation. The general population who request your free blessing will turn into your top prospects. Follow up with them to get bookings.

Chapter 4

Engaging Your Audience

Have you ever been in the crowd and listened to a speaker who just automatons on and on...? On the off chance that you have gone to school or worked in the corporate world, odds are you have. This is on account of in these situations; individuals are talked in light of their training, background, and position, not their capacity to talk. While it is incredible to have educated individuals speaking, the heartbreaking reaction is a group of people that is quite focusing, doesn't get the point, and may even nod off!

Talking is a work of art, and the capacity to keep a crowd of people drew in is basic to the speaker. One method of doing that is to utilize your voice as an instrument to attract the gathering of individuals. The word reference characterizes ramble as "to talk in a dull tone." Dull is marked as "told in an unvarying tone." Hence, on the off chance that you would prefer not to ramble on as a speaker, you should figure out how to change your tone.

Fluctuating your tone sounds sufficiently straightforward; simply stir up the volume, pitch, and speed of your discourse. The test is that while varying your tone sounds simple; it can be difficult to do. This happens for two reasons:

In our particular heads, when we talk, we have a tendency to hear how we think we sound. You may believe that you are shifting your voice a mess, however to a crowd of people you might be utterly dull.

You can wind up so centered around your substance and the words that you need to say that you may totally overlook or disregard the conveyance. This could be because of nerves, the absence of arrangement, unreliability, or numerous different things. In any case, once you disregard conveyance, you fall back on to whatever talking style you have dependably had. On the off chance that that happens to be a bit "ramble y," then you will exhaust your gathering of people.

The ultimate test is sufficiently simple to alter: Either record yourself talking and hear it out later (I know this can be agonizing. However it's precious!) or request original group of onlookers input from individuals you trust to give you legit yet valuable feedback. Joining a Toastmasters club is an incredible approach.

The second test is a considerable measure harder. How would you move some of your centers to conveyance when it's whatever you can do to control your apprehension and recall what you need to say next?

The primary path is to isolate content totally from the conveyance. To do this, utilization an improv drama method called "jabber." The drive is characterized as "confused or counter-intuitive talk." permanently, put on a show to convey an address, yet rather than communicating in English (or whatever your local tongue is), speak in babble. Make a progression of illogical sounds as you put on a show to address a crowd of people.

Now, your substance is superfluous. As you do this address, indeed play around with the velocity, volume, and pitch of your voice. While doing this, honestly go "over the top" with it. Keep in mind, in your head you presumably think your assortment is much greater than it is. By utilizing jabber, you can center 100% on your conveyance.

When you get a tiny bit agreeable only playing with the assortment in nonsense, you can take it up an indent with a fun accomplice exercise called the Rubbish Master:

You will be a specialist on some basic, ordinary point. You will then convey an address on this theme, yet you will talk just in babble. After each couple of sentences, respite, and let your accomplice "interpret" what you just said in babble. In execution, there are comedic contrivances to make this activity more entertaining (i.e. you talk in nonsense for 45 seconds, and your accomplice interprets with a solitary word like, "consequently"). With the end goal of learning vocal assortment, you would prefer not. The objective here is to get your accomplice to decipher as accurately as could reasonably be expected what you are stating, utilizing only your tone and voice. You will tend to use your hands and body; This is fine to some extent, however, don't transform this into a round of pretenses. You ought to convey your rubbish as though the group of onlookers comprehended you. By honing this, you will pick up a comprehension of how to utilize the tone of your voice to pass on as much data as the words you say.

Chapter 5

Promoting Your Business

We as a whole realize that informal exchange is the best and best promoting. Individuals encounter your administration or item, similar to what they experience and inform others regarding you. The main issue with this is it happens sporadically between two people or little gatherings along these lines taking a great deal longer the get the word out and construct your notoriety.

There is an approach to supercharging the informal procedure by getting significantly more individuals encountering your administration or item at one time, and it includes open talking. I know you would preferably kick the bucket than stand up before a gathering and talk. Be that as it may, stay with me and you very well might alter your opinion when you consider the advantages of advancing your business with open talking without expense to you.

Why is Open Speaking So Successful As a Business Special Apparatus?

It allows your group of onlookers to encounter your ability and your identity very close as it's been said. If they like what they hear and see and on the off chance that they feel an association with you they will either procure you and inform the world concerning you and your administration.

Step by step instructions to Continue

In each city, there are numerous affiliations, administration clubs, care groups, therapeutic services associations and so forth in critical need of speakers for their month to month gatherings or yearly feasts. Check your phone catalog or provincial group index distributed by your neighborhood daily paper for gathering names and contact data.

When you have chosen the gatherings you might want to present to, call them and request the name of the individual accountable for coating up speakers. They will be cheerful to get notification from you as their occupation is troublesome and they will value your offer to talk for nothing out of pocket.

1. Diagram your discussion to the individual accountable for getting speakers.

2. Push how your presentation will advantage their individuals.

3. Set up your display to take care of an issue for your audience members. Propose stable arrangements.

4. Put your presentation subject as a " How to" title.

Cases: How to Spook Confirmation Your Kids.

Five Approaches to Shield Your PC from Programmers

5. Try not to make your discussion excessively self-special. This will kill your gathering of people. Maybe a couple of references to your business amid your discussion will be okay. Abstain from having more than that.

6. Ensure you give extraordinary down to earth, useable data.

7. Suit your point to the gathering. If you have a PC administration business, and you are conversing with a P.T.A. bunch, an excellent talk would be " Ten Approaches to Shield Your Kids From Tyke Predators on the Web."

8. Be eager about your theme. Energy is infectious and influential.

9. Use cleverness inside your discussion. On the off chance that you can't recount a funny story then gather and utilize amusing jokes identified with your subject.

* To get a free duplicate of my 35Best Jokes mailto:oneliners@sendfree.com

10. Close to the end of your presentation welcomes your group of onlookers to get a duplicate of a tip sheet you arranged and conveyed with you identified with your subject. Toward the end of the tip sheet put your contact data in addition to an announcement welcoming them to duplicate the tip sheet and offer it to anybody they think would be intrigued. All you ask is that they copy the tip sheet as is with your contact data in thoughtfulness.

11. You can likewise show on the tip sheet and orally that you are accessible to address any gathering they think would profit by your message.

12. Have your business card and any pertinent limited time material as a component of a freebie for a group of onlookers individuals. Welcome, them to get a bundle before they clear out.

13. Toward the end of your discussion say, " I will be happy to stay around at the finish of the night to answer any inquiries you may have.

14. On the off chance that you have an on-line pamphlet or a different report identified with the point of the night offer to send them a duplicate if they would leave either their business card or their email address. When you return home to ensure you send them what you advertised. Make certain to keep their email addresses on the document for future contact.

15. If you are great, the word will spread, and you will begin inspiring calls to talk. When this happens, you can start charging an expense for your talking administrations.

When I started charging for my talking policies, I did 50 in one year for $200 per discourse. Presently I do 40 or 50 a year for amongst $1800 and $2500 in addition to costs. I get generously compensated to talk regardless I profit from verbal promoting.

Conclusion

On the off chance that you have a trepidation of open talking don't give it a chance to prevent you from profiting from the limited time benefit of giving presentations. Recall that you just beat your fears by defying them head on. When you vanquish your apprehension of talking openly, you will have available to you an intense and viable reputation apparatus. Also, you won't have top pay out one penny.

Chapter 6

Developing Confidence

On the off chance that you are talking before a gathering, paying little respect to how or why you arrived, you are a specialist. The whole crowd is taking a gander at you as the individual who knows enough about the subject to be requested that talk. Accordingly, you should introduce yourself as a specialist (not as a matter of course "the" master, but rather "a" specialist) There are two approaches to present yourself as an expert: 1)know your material and 2)project certainty.

Knowing your stuff is self-evident. If you are addressing a gathering, you should take in your article and take as much time as you have to get ready.

Certainty is trickier because certainty is a psyche diversion. It is not extraordinary, be that as it may, for amazingly ill-equipped individuals to venture certainty and for to a significant degree arranged speakers to extend a conspicuous absence of certainty.

The objective is to organize and reach confidence. In any case, you might be arranged and still feel unstable. This could be because of a general trepidation of talking, weight from the size or make-up of the group of onlookers, shakiness in light of different speakers, or numerous different reasons. Notwithstanding the reason, you should have the capacity to set it aside and make the gathering of people trust that you are sure.

So how would you anticipate certainty notwithstanding when you have none? The key boils down to one critical point:

"You don't need to be certain; you need to venture certainty."

While your long haul objective is to be sure, in the transient you just need to take charge of the phase in a way that makes the gathering of people trust you are confident.

The most natural and quickest approach to doing this is to control your body. Attempt the accompanying four things:

Stand up straight. Nothing extends instability like a man who is somewhat slouched over or looking down. Keep in mind the stance lessons from your childhood! Envision a string from the most noteworthy point on your head delicately pulling your body up. Presently envision the line giving up and unwind your body - yet don't fall back and let your body break down - hold your upright, stable position.

Open your body up. The most simple way speakers venture unreliability is by shutting their bodies off. This comes through breaking down the body in, intersection arms (or placing them in your pockets), dismissing marginally from the gathering of people, or holding up behind the platform. When you stand up straight, attempt to keep your body open to the group of individuals.

Venture your voice. This will take rehearse. The most particular speaker on the planet will sound powerless if the panel of people can not hear them. Furthermore, your message will be lost if the group of onlookers needs to battle to hear you. Rehearse the specialty of serenely extending your voice so that the whole room can hear you. A little voice is connected with shakiness; a high sound ventures certainty, regardless of the possibility that the speaker is terrified out of his minds!

Moderate down. Unless you have an especially very lively frantic style, talking and moving rapidly will make a picture of frailty. The vast majority speed up when they feel frightened. It's as though they are attempting to complete their discourse as fast as could be allowed so they can get off the stage. Try to back off both your conveyance and developments, and you will extend a particular picture to the group of onlookers.

Chapter 7

Special Guest Speakers

Lawmakers, VIP's and VIP speakers frequently hope to carry their life partner or an assistant with them when they travel. On the off chance that different gatherings are included ensure you have something in composing that diagrams what the comprehension is on hotel and nourishment repayment. If you hold your speaker's administrations well ahead of time of your gathering date, he or she might have the capacity to mastermind different engagements near your meeting date and area.

If you want your speaker to go to get-togethers before or after the presentation, make certain, the speaker knows about your solicitation well ahead of time. Much of the time a speaker will invest the energy just before his/her presentation gets ready to go on the stage. Speakers are cheerful to go to additional occasions if given adequate notification. Know, nonetheless, that a few speakers incline toward not to go to get-togethers and some charge additional for any extra time spent.

Make sure to get the speaker's photo and anecdotal data to guarantee you have what you requirement for any productions (programs, handouts, pamphlets). The speaker will likewise give you a suitable presentation.

Send the speaker however much data as could be expected about your association including organization pamphlets, yearly reports, and any significant meeting announcements. Likewise, send the speaker duplicates of any material specifying his or her presentation.

Numerous speakers and workshop pioneers have composed books and delivered tape tapes of their projects. Make a standard comprehension about what advancement of their materials will be permitted.

Notice of items being accessible can be done promptly taking after a speaker's presentation. Participants frequently profit by material that develops the estimation of the performance. If you need to make an audiotape or tape of a presentation make certain to get marked approval ahead of time.

1. Check contracts for settlement prerequisites.

2. Bars, snacks and complimentary smorgasbords.

3. Transportation - to and from the occasion and to and from the air terminal - limousines, helicopters, private planes.

4. Welcome, and neighborliness game plans to set up.

5. Reference material about association supplied to speaker well ahead of time.

6. The framework of discourse got the previous occasion.

7. The date was given for when life story, headshot and Prolog to be gotten.

8. Courses of action for some other person(s) going to the speaker.

9. Know about VIP's inclinations i.e. likes to golf, will go to the feast, meet and welcome.

10. Convey thank you letters.

11. Blessings - either conveyed to room amid meeting, introduced taking after discourse or sent after the occasion.

12. Permit time for inquiries from the group of onlookers taking after speaker's presentation

Chapter 8

Losing The Fear Of Public Speaking

Obviously, it's not simply you. Everybody is petrified at the very considered talking before a gathering of their related individuals. Which implies that this apprehension is characteristic. Humankind is alarmed of its kind.

Why would it be advisable for this to be? The response to that question lies in ancient times; as make the responses to some different inquiries in regards to our responses to individuals. So let us backtrack - back to the season of the cave dwellers. There we will meet Ug - a powerful seeker.

Ug and his colleagues vanished centuries back naturally. However, we as a whole have a tiny bit of him in us right up 'til the present time. In our qualities. We are the children and girls of Ug, and we demonstrate this in our natural responses at the most fundamental level. So we should remember one day quite a while back.

A decent day for chasing

It was a perfect, sunny day. Ideal for chasing. Furthermore, that was exactly what Ug had as the top priority. He was setting off on a chasing endeavor. He took up his most loved dance and set off towards the backwoods where he knew he ought to locate a fat deer or other little amusement.

He hadn't gone far when, abruptly, up ahead, he saw a gathering of stone age men. They were not from his more distant family and in this manner, in those brutal days, they spoke to a potential threat.

Quickly he spotted them, a couple of little endocrine organs, arranged directly over Ug's kidneys, started to emit an effective hormone - adrenaline. As the medication sped through his circulatory system, Ug's heartbeat rate stimulated, his face flushed, his mouth got to be dry, and he started to shake. Risk undermined, and Ug was anxious! His body was setting itself up for battle, or escaping.

Had they seen him? Should he run, or would he be better attempting to mix into the view until they had gone on? He dropped to the ground behind a little hedge and squeezed his face into the earth, trusting the outsiders would not hear the beating of his heart or the scratching of his breath.

Fortunate getaway

Fortunes were with Ug that day, and the gathering went by without seeing him. In the wake of holding up a while to make sure they had gone, Ug set off again and soon achieved the woodland. He crawled through the trees; all his detects alarm. He could travel through the timberland noiselessly; his feeling of smell was extents more touchy than advanced man's, and his responses were those of a top of the line competitor. To be sure, he was a top of the line competitor.

In the long run, he went to a clearing. Remaining on the opposite side of the clearing stood a beautiful, fat deer. Exactly what Ug had been seeking after.

Quickly he recognized the deer, a couple of little endocrine organs, arranged simply over Ug's kidneys, started to discharge a powerful hormone - adrenaline. As the medication sped through his circulatory system, Ug's heartbeat rate stimulated, his face flushed, his mouth got to be dry, and he started to shake. The chase was on, and Ug was energized! His lance arm snapped back, and he heaved the weapon over the clearing with lightning speed. His point was valid; straight to the heart of the deer rushed his rocket. The creature dropped dead in a split second. Ug hung it over his shoulders and took his execute home. Luckily he didn't meet any more outsiders in transit and, that night, the entire family had a superb banquet. Ugh, the considerable seeker, was, actually, the visitor of honor and was required to make an after supper discourse. Instantly he confronted talk, a couple of little endocrine organs, arranged simply over Ug's kidneys, started to emit a capable hormone - adrenaline. As the medication sped through his circulation system, Ug's heartbeat rate revived, his face flushed, his mouth got to be dry, and he started to shake. Ug felt precisely the way you and I do under comparable circumstances! Is it safe to say that he was panicked? On the other hand energized?

The point to see here is that Ug's physiological responses to risk (dread) and excite (energy) were precisely the same. As are yours and mine and each other human beings.

Enter the adoration interest!

Of course, in the wake of making a fruitful discourse (comprising to a large degree of snorts) Ug went for a stroll in the social affair sunset. Over the span of his walk, he stumbled upon a cave lady. To us she would have looked mainly like Ug - however to him, she was exceptionally alluring.

Instantly he detected her, a couple of little endocrine organs, arranged directly over Ug's kidneys, started to emit a capable hormone - adrenaline. As the medication sped through his circulation system, Ug's heartbeat rate stimulated, his face flushed, his mouth got to be dry, and he started to shake.

The truth is out - the very same physiological side effects.

What does it mean?

As such, so what? Two things:

One, we have no influence over how we respond physiologically. Remaining before a gathering spells risk, as it has. In dangerous circumstances, individuals get sweat-soaked and flimsy. Chasing is energizing. In energizing times, individuals get sweat-soaked and unsteady. A few people from the opposite sex are exceptionally alluring. When we discover individuals incredibly appealing, we are inclined to end up sweat-soaked and unstable. The same reaction yet to several jolts.

Two, in a talking circumstance, nobody knows, unless you let them know, whether you are terrified of them or energized at the possibility of conversing with them! You don't know either - until you start breaking down the circumstance mentally. I prescribe consequently that you receive this methodology:

Let yourself know that you are energized!

At that point tell your group of onlookers that you are so eager to address them! That way, if they see your handshake as you reach for the water container, or spot a flush to your cheek as you talk, they're complimented! "Gosh, (s)he is energized, (s)he's not trying to say it!"

Furthermore, prepare to have your mind blown. If you let yourself know and your crowd how energized you are frequently enough, you may even come to trust it yourself.

www.ingramcontent.com/pod-product-compliance
Lightning Source LLC
Chambersburg PA
CBHW070423190526
45169CB00003B/1389